SECRET AGENT

TRAINING MANUAL

P9-CEM-506

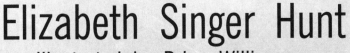

HOW TO MAKE AND BREAK TOP SECRET MESSAGES

Elizabeth Singer Hunt

Illustrated by Brian Williamson

WEINSTEIN
BOOKS

Copyright © 2017 by Elizabeth Singer Hunt

Illustrations copyright © 2017 by Brian Williamson

All rights reserved. No part of this book may be used or reproduced in any manner whatsoever without the written permission of the Publisher. For information address Weinstein Books, 1290 Avenue of the Americas, New York, NY 10104.

Printed in the United States of America.

Cataloging-in-Publication data for this book is available from the Library of Congress.

ISBN: 978-1-60286-339-2 (print)
ISBN: 978-1-60286-340-8 (e-book)

Published by Weinstein Books
A member of Hachette Book Group
www.weinsteinbooks.com

Weinstein Books are available at special discounts for bulk purchases in the U.S. by corporations, institutions and other organizations. For more information, please contact the Special Markets Department at Perseus Books, 2300 Chestnut Street, Suite 200, Philadelphia, PA 19103, call (800) 810-4145, ext. 5000, or e-mail special.markets@perseusbooks.com.

First edition

LSC-C

10 9 8 7 6 5 4 3 2 1

For Corinne, my inspiration.

A WORD ABOUT THIS BOOK

Imagine that you're a secret agent. You have to send a message to a fellow spy. How can you disguise it so that the enemy can't read it? You can use "cryptography," or the art of hiding top secret messages.

Inside are more than twenty-five techniques for keeping *your* top secret messages private. You'll learn how to make invisible ink, create unbreakable ciphers, communicate in code, and craft your own decoder gadgets. You'll even have a chance to test your newfound skills by deciphering the "Cryptographic Challenge" at the end of the book.

Above all, have fun! Even if you're not interested in becoming a secret agent, you can use the tips and tricks learned in this manual to exchange top secret notes with your friends.

Elizabeth Singer Hunt

HISTORY OF CRYPTOGRAPHY

STEGANOGRAPHY

CIPHERS

CODES

CRYPTOGRAPHIC CHALLENGE

HISTORY OF CRYPTOGRAPHY

HISTORY OF CRYPTOGRAPHY

For thousands of years, people have used "cryptography," or the art of hiding top secret messages. Some of the earliest examples of cryptography can be found in the writings of the ancient Greeks.

Herodotus

FUN FACT: The word "cryptography" has Greek origins. KRYPTOS means "hidden," and GRAPHEIN means "writing."

More than 2,400 years ago (during the fifth century B.C.), a well-known historian named Herodotus sent a note to his fellow Greeks that the Persian army was about to attack. He did this by concealing his message on a wooden writing tablet covered in wax. Once the wax was scraped off, his message was revealed.

Around the same time, another Greek named Histiaeus reportedly used a man's head to send his message. He shaved the man's scalp, tattooed the message on it, waited for the man's hair to grow back, and then sent the man off to deliver the note. Other Greeks were known to stuff their messages in the bodies of dead animals. This kind of cryptography—when communications are hidden in or on something—is called "steganography."

FUN FACT: The word "steganography" comes from the Greek words STEGANOS meaning "covered" and GRAPHEIN meaning "to write."

But the ancient Greeks weren't the only ones to use steganography. The ancient Chinese used it too. Sometimes they scribbled their secret messages on parchment, rolled them up, and coated them in wax. Many of these wax "balls" were delivered as is. Other times, they were further hidden by swallowing them. They were only revealed when they came out the other end. Yuck!

While the Greeks and Chinese were using steganography, the ancient Romans were finding new ways of concealing their messages. After all, hiding notes on people's heads and in dead animals wasn't always that reliable.

So, the Romans decided to try their luck with ciphers. A "cipher" is a type of cryptic communication that relies on substituting the letters of the normal alphabet with letters of a made-up "cipher alphabet." If the cipher was seized, it would be hard for the enemy to decipher it. That is, unless he or she knew the rule or "key" to figuring it out.

One of the most famous Romans to use ciphers was Julius Caesar. Caesar was a Roman general who conquered territories for Rome. Because he was constantly sending messages back and forth, he needed a way of keeping his communications safe. The cipher alphabet that Caesar came up with used letters that were three places to the right of the normal alphabet. Instead of writing an "A," Caesar used a "D." For "B" he wrote an "E," and so on.

Julius Caesar
(100–44 BC)

TRY THIS: Try writing a Caesar cipher for the word "HI."
Write down the letter three spaces to the right of "H," and
then "I." If you came up with "KL," you're correct!
Congratulations, you've just written your first Caesar cipher.

In addition to ciphers, the Romans were working on other ways to conceal their messages. A scientist named Pliny the Elder discovered that the juice of the tithymalus plant made an excellent invisible ink. Because the juice dried almost clear, it was difficult to read. The only way to see the message was to hold it up to a heat source—like a fire—and wait for the writing to oxidize or turn brown.

During the thirteenth century A.D., a Franciscan friar named Roger Bacon wrote a book that taught people to disguise their messages.

Bacon developed a kind of cipher that used a combination of As and Bs to represent the letters of the normal alphabet. The letter "A" was written as "AAAA," and the letter "C" was written as "AABA." It was a "binary" system of writing because a combination of two letters ("A" and "B") was used to communicate the entire twenty-six-letter alphabet.

By the sixteenth century A.D., the ability to write and crack codes had become an important survival skill, especially among those in power. After all, people were always plotting to overthrow them. Monarchs, popes, and the ruling families of Europe had secretaries or "spymasters" in their inner circle. It was the spymaster's job to intercept and crack ciphers that were being sent between adversaries.

In 1586, the skills of Sir Francis Walsingham (the spymaster for Queen Elizabeth I of England) and his team of cryptanalysts were tested.

Mary, Queen of Scots, was the queen of Scotland. She was also Elizabeth I's cousin. Many felt that Mary, instead of Elizabeth, was the rightful heir to the English throne. To protect herself and her power, Elizabeth imprisoned Mary in a home in England called Chartley Hall.

While Mary was at Chartley Hall, a man named Sir Anthony Babington sent her a

Mary, Queen of Scots

Sir Francis Walsingham

cipher written on paper hidden in a beer barrel. He told Mary about his plan to free her, assassinate Elizabeth, and make Mary queen of England. After reading the letter, Mary wrote back to Babington using a cipher too, telling him that she approved of Elizabeth's assassination.

Unfortunately for Babington and Mary, Elizabeth's spymaster, Walsingham, got a hold of the notes, and his cryptographer easily deciphered the ciphers. Mary, Babington, and the other conspirators were charged with treason and executed.

Blaise de Vigenère

At the same time of Mary's demise, the art of cryptography was spreading across continental Europe. More and more people were practicing with ciphers, and it was becoming more difficult to develop one that was unbreakable.

In 1586, a French man named Blaise de Vigenère took a crack at developing an unbreakable cipher. He based it on a table that he created, which used different permutations of a Caesar cipher combined with a keyword. It was ingenious. Without a copy of Vigenère's table, his ciphers were difficult to break.

In the 1700s, secret societies of men in England, Scotland, and Europe (like the Rosicrucians and Freemasons) developed their own style of writing. This secret writing was based on symbols created by the placement of letters and dots on a collection of four grids. Since two of these grids look like a tic-tac-toe board, ciphers are called "tic-tac-toe" ciphers.

Around the same time, European countries started to build teams of people called "bureaus" or "cabinets," whose purpose was to spy on other people's letters. Some of these groups had dark names like the "Black Chamber."

The most famous was the Viennese Black Chamber of Austria. They would open envelopes, make copies of the letters inside, and, if need be, decode the ciphers and then seal the envelope back up with an identical wax seal.

CLASSIFIED

In the Americas, the use of cryptography was just beginning. Benjamin Franklin used ciphers during the Revolutionary War (1775–1783), while the future first president of the United States, George Washington, relied on invisible ink to write his messages.

In 1795, American Thomas Jefferson created the idea of a code wheel for writing ciphers that had thirty-six numbered discs on it. Each of the discs had the twenty-six letters of the alphabet, and could move on their own. The fact that the discs could be randomly ordered meant that the ciphers made from the wheel would have been difficult to solve.

In 1832, an American man named Samuel Morse came up with the idea of a single-wire electric telegraph. Electric telegraphs that transmitted impulses over multiple wires had been around for many years. But Morse's telegraph was different. His used only one wire, and was cheaper to make. Soon, Morse's version of the telegraph became the standard for the world.

George Washington

Samuel Morse
(1791–1872 A.D.)

A Telegraph

The reason that Morse is included in this history of cryptography is not because of his telegraph, but because of the "code" that he developed to go along with it. Morse needed a way to spell letters with the sounds that the telegraph made. The telegraph could make a short "dit" sound if you tapped on it quickly. Or, it could make a longer "dah" sound if you held it down longer.

So, Morse and a couple of other men developed combinations of "dits" and "dahs" to represent individual letters. Written down, the "dit" sound was represented by a dot, while the "dah" sound was represented by a dash.

In 1918, a German inventor named Arthur Scherbius patented an idea for a rotor machine that could create complex ciphers. The discs inside would rotate. Scherbius's machine was later improved and eventually became known as the "Enigma."

The Enigma was similar to Jefferson's wheel cipher, but more sophisticated. It used electricity. Every time you pushed a button, the electrical contacts would activate the wheels and they would rotate. Because the wheels were constantly turning, a different key or solution for each letter was introduced to the cipher.

During World War II, the Germans relied on the Enigma to disguise their messages. Other countries involved in the war also developed their own cipher machines. The Americans used the SIGABA. The British had the TYPEX, and the Japanese used their TYPE 97 machine. The Americans nicknamed the Japanese machine "Purple."

Enigma Machine

The Enigma, however was one of the toughest to crack. That's why a top secret code-breaking bureau was created in England at Bletchley Park.

Eventually the codebreakers deciphered some of the Enigma's ciphers. The Bletchley Park cryptanalysts were credited with helping to defeat Adolf Hitler and shortening the length of the war by two years.

Beyond the machines, other methods of cryptography were used during World War II. Invisible ink was used, codes were sewn into scarves and clothing, and messages were hidden under postage stamps.

In the last sixty years, big advances have been made in cryptography. Computers have replaced machines like the Enigma as the number one source for developing and cracking complex codes and ciphers. Even today, computers are used around the world to encrypt and decipher important data.

Steganography involves hiding top secret messages in or on something else. In ancient times, the Greeks and Romans delivered their messages in the bellies of dead animals and under the hair on people's heads. In recent times, secret agent communications have been hidden on pieces of clothing and on microdots.

In this section, you'll learn twelve easy ways to hide your messages using steganography. The neat thing about steganography is that you don't have to change the message itself. All you have to do is come up with a clever way for delivering it.

FUN FACT: A microdot is a miniature message or photo imprinted on a tiny disc. The messages are so small (about the size of the period at the end of this sentence) that you need a microscope to read them.

1. MAKING AND USING INVISIBLE INK

Almost two thousand years ago, a Roman author and naturalist named Pliny the Elder discovered that the juice of the tithymalus plant made an excellent invisible ink. Because the juice dried almost clear, it was difficult to read. The only way to read the message was to hold it up to a heat source—like a fire—and wait for the writing to oxidize or turn brown.

Since a tithymalus plant is hard to come by, here's another way to make invisible ink. Like the plant, this recipe creates an "ink" that nearly disappears. But it doesn't need heat or fire to show the message. It can safely be revealed by using dark fruit juice.

Pliny the Elder
(23-79 AD)

HERE'S WHAT YOU'LL NEED:

1) 2 tablespoons or 30 ml of baking soda (also known as sodium bicarbonate)

2) 2 tablespoons or 30 ml of water

3) 4 tablespoons or 60 ml of dark fruit juice like grape or cranberry juice

4) 2 small bowls

5) 1 cotton swab, paintbrush, or toothpick

6) 1 cotton ball (a paper towel also works)

7) White paper

FUN FACT: Sometimes when spies run out of invisible ink, they use their own urine to write their messages. YUCK!

HERE'S HOW TO DO IT:

Put the baking soda and water in a bowl and mix them together. (This is your invisible ink.) Dip your cotton swab, toothpick, or paintbrush into the ink and use it to write your message on the white paper. You'll need to let your message dry for at least 20 minutes.

When you're ready to reveal your message, put the fruit juice into the other bowl and lightly dip the cotton ball (or paper towel) into the juice. Gently rub the cotton ball over your invisible ink message. As soon as the juice touches the invisible ink, your message will magically appear!

Use only a bit of juice

TIP: Make sure your friend or fellow agent knows the "juicy" secret to revealing the message beforehand, or else they won't be able to read it. And never, EVER taste any of the recipes in this book! They're disgusting and might actually harm you.

2. OTHER FORMS OF INVISIBLE INK

If you don't have the ingredients for the previous invisible ink recipe, you can always use a leftover birthday candle or white-colored pencil.

HERE'S WHAT YOU'LL NEED:

1) 1 light-colored birthday candle OR 1 white-colored pencil
2) 1 dark-colored crayon (preferably dark purple, red, or dark blue)
3) Plain paper

HERE'S HOW TO DO IT:

Use your light-colored candle or white pencil to write your message on the paper. Make sure that you push down hard enough and write against a flat surface.

To reveal your message, VERTICALLY color over it with your darker-colored crayon. In other words, color it up and down, not side to side. Your message will show up better that way.

KEEP OUT

Color up and down

TIP: Of the two, the birthday candle will work best because the wax candle is thicker and will coat the paper better than the pencil, which will only leave a thin indentation.

3. USING BACKWARD SPELLING

One of the easiest ways to hide your message is to spell it backward.

HERE'S WHAT YOU'LL NEED:

1) 1 pen, pencil, or marker
2) Plain paper

HERE'S HOW TO DO IT:

First, decide what you want to say. Scribble your message on a sheet of paper. As an example, I am going to send the following message:

BEING A SECRET AGENT IS FUN

To encode it, all I have to do is spell each word backward.

GNIEB A TERCES TNEGA SI NUF

It's as simple as that! As long as your fellow friend or agent knows the key to solving it, he or she will be able to easily decode it.

If you wanted to make it trickier to solve, you could insert a "null." A null is a letter, number, or symbol that has nothing to do with the message itself. Its only purpose is to visually confuse someone. Take a look at how tricky my message looks when I insert the number 4 before each word.

4GNIEB 4A 4TERCES 4TNEGA 4SI 4NUF

Now THAT'S a complicated-looking message!

To decode it, all I would have to do is scratch out the nulls and reverse the spelling.

CRACK THE CODE!

See if you can use your new skills to crack these backward-coded messages. If you get stuck, you can always find the answers in the "Answer Key" at the back of the book.

OD UOY EVAH RUOY YPS SESSALG = _____

_____

EKAM ERUS OT RAEW PUEKAM = _____

_____

TAHW EMIT LLIW EHT EGAKCAP EVIRRA = _____

_____

TI SI NEDDIH EDISNI EHT NEP = _____

_____

ESU ELBISIVNI KNI = _____

_____

TIP: To make your message even harder to decipher, you could also write the sentence backward in addition to the spelling. For example, BEING A SECRET AGENT IS FUN would be encrypted as:

NUF SI TNEGA TERCES A GNIEB

As always, you'll want to tell your friend or fellow agent the key to solving it, i.e. the words and sentences are spelled backward, so that he or she can easily decode it.

4. MAKING AND USING A SCYTALE

A "scytale" (pronounced ski-tally) is the name of an ancient cylindrical tool used to create and decipher messages. The Greeks used scytales thousands of years ago as a way to disguise their communications during military campaigns. Back then, they used wood to make the cylinder and leather straps to write their messages. But you don't need wood and leather. You can make a scytale using recycled goods from around your house.

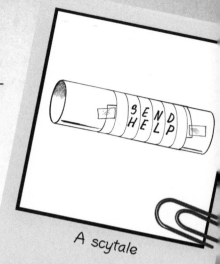

A scytale

HERE'S WHAT YOU'LL NEED:

1) 1 brown tube from inside a roll of paper towels
2) 1 ruler
3) Scissors
4) Clear tape
5) A pen, marker, or pencil to write with
6) Plain paper

HERE'S HOW TO DO IT:

Cut a sheet of paper into several long, thin strips. Try to make each strip the same width (ideally about ½ in or 1 cm wide). Once your strips are cut, tape the ends of the strips together to form one long band of paper.

Tape one end of the paper to the end of the brown tube. MAKE SURE THAT THE PAPER IS TAPED AT A SLIGHT ANGLE. Then, wrap the paper around and around—keeping the edges close together but not overlapping each other—until you run out of paper or reach the end of the tube. Cut off the excess paper and fasten the end of the paper to the tube with tape.

Wrap the paper
at an angle

Write one letter per strip

Now it's time to write your message. Do it from left to right, using only one letter per strip. You can even write it over multiple lines like in this example.

When you're finished, detach the strip of paper from the tube. Notice how the paper has a list of random letters with spaces in between that don't make any sense. That's the genius of a scytale! Unless someone has an identical device, they will have no idea how to put the letters together to form a message.

To decode a scytale message, tape one end of the paper to the scytale at an angle and wrap it around and around, keeping the edges of the paper close together. If you've done it correctly, you should be able to see your original message again.

TIP: If you're writing a message to a friend or fellow agent, make sure that he or she has the same sized tube. Never send your message already attached to the tube!

5. USING MIRROR WRITING

Try and read this message.

THIS IS A BACKWARDS MESSAGE. BOTH
THE LETTERS AND THE ORDER OF THE
LETTERS ARE WRITTEN BACKWARDS.

Not as easy as reading it the right way around, huh? Now, hold it up to a mirror.

See what happened?

When the light hit the mirror, it bounced back, so that the message was reversed and easy to read. This type of writing is called "mirror writing." But mirror writing isn't just about spelling words backward. It's about writing the letters backward too.

Mirrors can reverse writing

HERE'S WHAT YOU'LL NEED:

1) 1 dark ink pen or marker
2) Plain paper

HERE'S HOW TO DO IT:

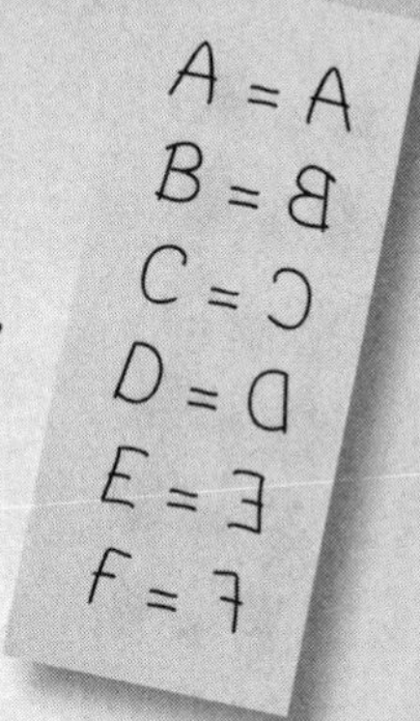

First, practice writing the letters of the alphabet backward. To do this, write the letters in such a way that they face the **opposite** direction of what they normally do. Here's what the alphabet would look like if the letters were written backward.

A = A
B = B
C = C
D = D
E = E
F = F

ABCDEFGHIJKLMNOP
QRSTUVWXYZ
(written backward, right to left)

Notice that I have written it from right to left. That way, when you hold it up to the mirror, it will reverse itself to what's normal: left to right. Lucky for us, many of the letters ("A," "H," "M," "N," "O," "T," "U," "V," "W," and "X") look the same backward as they do forward.

Let's go back to the original message.

THIS IS A BACKWARDS MESSAGE. BOTH
THE LETTERS AND THE ORDER OF THE
LETTERS ARE WRITTEN BACKWARDS.
(written backward)

To write your own backward message, all you have to do is write it from right to left, making sure to write your letters in the opposite direction. Try practicing writing your own message now.

The only problem with backward writing is that some people can read it without a mirror. So, if you're sending a backward message, you'll need to include tricks to make it tougher to decipher.

Once again, you could use a null. Remember, a null is a number, symbol, or letter that has nothing to do with the message itself.

For my null, I have inserted a 6. See how my message already looks more confusing?

THIS6 IS6 A6 BACKWARDS6 MESSAGE.6
BOTH6 THE6 LETTERS6 AND6 THE6
ORDER6 OF6 THE6 LETTERS6 ARE6
WRITTEN6 BACKWARDS.6

Now, take a look at what happens when I add a second null—the letter "Z" after the 6. (If you're going to use a letter as your null, make sure it's not already in your message.)

THIS6Z IS6Z A6Z BACKWARDS6Z MESSAGE.6Z
BOTH6Z THE6Z LETTERS6Z AND6Z THE6Z
ORDER6Z OF6Z THE6Z LETTERS6Z ARE6Z
WRITTEN6Z BACKWARDS.6Z

If you wanted to make it even harder, you could write your message really small.

THIS6Z IS6Z A6Z BACKWARDS6Z MESSAGE.6Z
BOTH6Z THE6Z LETTERS6Z AND6Z THE6Z
ORDER6Z OF6Z THE6Z LETTERS6Z ARE6Z
WRITTEN6Z BACKWARDS.6Z

To solve a mirror message, all you have to do is scratch out the nulls and hold it up to the mirror.

THIS6Z IS6Z A6Z BACKWARDS6Z MESSAGE.6Z
BOTH6Z THE6Z LETTERS6Z AND6Z THE6Z
ORDER6Z OF6Z THE6Z LETTERS6Z ARE6Z
WRITTEN6Z BACKWARDS.6Z

TIP: Writing with darker ink is best because lighter colors are harder to see in the mirror.

24

CRACK THE CODE!

Below is a message written in mirror writing. See if you can figure out what it says. The nulls are X and 3.

BEING3 AX3 SECRET3 AGENT3 IS3
DANGEROUSX BUT3 IT3 CAN3
ALSO3 BE3 LOTS3 OF3 FUN.3

Try and write the following phrase as a mirror message: SECRET AGENT TRAINING INVOLVES LEARNING HOW TO CRACK CODES.

6. USING THE "BUMP AND SHIFT"

Another way to hide a message is to "bump" the last letter of each word to the right, and "shift" the spacing between words to the left. Although these sorts of messages look complex, it's just visual trickery.

HERE'S WHAT YOU'LL NEED:

1) 1 pen, pencil, or marker
2) Plain paper

HERE'S HOW TO DO IT:

First, write your message on a sheet of paper in capital letters. As an example, I am going to send the following message:

BEWARE OF THE OLD MAN

Second, bump the last letter of each word to become the first letter of the next, and then shift the spacing to the left by one.

BEWAR EO FTH EOL DMA N

Depending upon your message, you might be happy to stop there. But if you wanted to add another level of security, you could add a null. Here's my message with a null of 3.

3BEWAR 3EO 3FTH 3EOL 3DMA 3N

To solve a bump-and-shift message, all you have to do is scratch out the nulls and then do the reverse. Bump the first letter of each word to the left and shift the spacing over one to the right.

3BEWAR 3EO 3FTH 3EOL 3DMA 3N

CRACK THE CODE!

Now that you understand how to use the "bump and shift" method, you can practice your skills by deciphering the following coded messages. Look out for nulls! Hint: The nulls in the last three messages are numbers.

TH EP APER SAR EI NTH EBRIEFCAS E = _____

_____

H EI S ARUSSIA NSP Y = _____

_____

8SH 8EWIL 8LMEE 8TYO 8UI 8NTH 8EPAR 8K = _____

_____

2TH 2EPLAN 2EWIL 2LLAN 2DA 2T7 = _____

_____

2TRAININ 2GSTART 2SA 2T1 21 = _____

_____

7. HIDING YOUR MESSAGE IN A MAGAZINE ARTICLE

An age-old spy trick is to hide a message on a page from a book, newspaper, or magazine. Since newspapers are harder to come by these days, we're going to use a page from an old magazine.

HERE'S WHAT YOU'LL NEED:

1) 1 page from a used magazine. Make sure there are several stories on it.
2) 1 pen or pencil
3) Plain paper

HERE'S HOW TO DO IT:

First, think of what you want to say and scribble your message on a sheet of scratch paper. I'm going to use the following as an example.

MEET ME AT THE LUNCH TABLES

Next, as you read your magazine article, use your pencil to put a light dot underneath each letter that spells the words in your message. Make sure that the letters are marked in the exact order as they appear in your message.

Here's how I marked the letters of my message in the article.

BEST AND BRIGHTEST OLYMPIC HOPEFULS
By Olympia Gold

GYMNASTIC SUPERSTAR, Natalya Korchenko has broken all records. Not only is the twelve-year-old the youngest gymnast ever to enter the Olympics, she's also the smallest. She stands at only 4 feet 3 inches tall. Her parents are extremely proud of her and are crossing fingers that she carries home the gold for Russia.

IN OTHER NEWS, the Jamaican bobsledding team is gearing up for their next appearance in the winter Olympics in Japan. Can they defend their gold medal title? Only time will tell.

To decode this message, all you have to do is write down the letters with the dots in the order that they appear.

MEETMEATTHELUNCHTABLES

Even though there are no spaces, you can still understand what the message is trying to communicate.

> TIP: Instead of dots, you could also try lightly underlining your letters. Or, use a highlighter, although this will make your message more obvious.

29

8. HIDING YOUR MESSAGE IN A HANDWRITTEN NOTE

If a magazine is hard to find, you could always conceal your message in a handwritten note. Handwritten notes are great because people usually don't look past what's written to see if there's something else lurking behind the letters.

HERE'S WHAT YOU'LL NEED:

1) 1 pencil, pen, or collection of colored markers
2) Plain paper

HERE'S HOW TO DO IT:

First, scribble your message on a scratch sheet of paper. You're going to use this to refer to later. As an example, I am going to hide the following message in my note.

WATCH OUT

Second, come up with a fake topic to talk about. I've decided to tell my parents about my day at school. (Clearly, I'm not going to send this to my parents. It's just a fake note that I'm going to deliver to my fellow friend or agent.)

If someone were to see it, they would think it was an ordinary note. But look closer. While most of the letter was written using lowercase letters, there are some suspicious uppercase or capital letters. These capital letters spell my message.

dear mom and dad,

i Wish you could hAve seen me aT school today! i sCored a goal during recess and even got a good grade in matH. i lOve school becaUse iT's so much fun!

lots of love,

elizabeth

To decode the message, all I have to do is write down the capital letters in the order that they appeared.

WATCHOUT

Even without spaces, the message is clear.

The key to hiding a message in a fake letter is to choose a method for making the letters of the message stand out, but in a way that's not too obvious. I chose to use capital letters, but you might choose to use different colors.

TIP #1: Make sure to tell your friend and fellow agent the key to solving your message beforehand such as "capital letters" or "red letters."

TIP #2: In addition to using capital letters and colors, you could also bold the letters, lighten them, or put dots underneath. See what other ways you can come up with to disguise your message in a handwritten note.

9. HIDING YOUR MESSAGE IN A CROSSWORD PUZZLE

Empty crossword puzzles are excellent vehicles for hiding top secret messages. Plus, they're easy to find. You can download them from the internet or rip them out of an old magazine. If you want to send a long message, make sure to choose a puzzle with lots of squares.

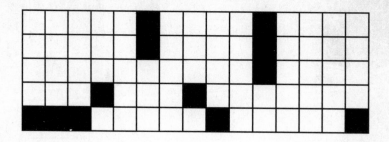

HERE'S WHAT YOU'LL NEED:

1) 1 unused crossword puzzle
2) 1 pen, pencil, or marker

HERE'S HOW TO DO IT:

First, decide what message you want to send. As an example, I am going to send the message THE PRESIDENT ARRIVES AT NOON.

Second, come up with a null. Since Z isn't used in the message, THE PRESIDENT ARRIVES AT NOON, it makes a good null.

Write your null in the upper left-hand square of the crossword grid. Moving left to right, fill in the rest of the squares with your message adding a null in between each word.

If you have a short message, not all of the squares will be used. So, you can either fill the remaining squares with random letters. Or, you can repeat the message over and over again.

Here's an example of what my crossword puzzle looks like with the message THE PRESIDENT ARRIVES AT NOON.

Z	T	H	E	Z	■	P	R	E	S	■	I	D	E	N
T	Z	A	R	R	■	I	V	E	S	■	Z	A	T	Z
N	O	O	N	Z	T	H	E	Z	P	■	R	E	S	I
D	E	N	■	T	Z	A	■	R	R	I	V	E	S	Z
■	A	T	Z	N	O	■	O	N	Z	T	H	■		

To solve it, all my fellow agent would have to do is scratch out the nulls.

10. HIDING SNAIL MAIL MESSAGES

Pretend that you need to send a message to a fellow spy in another country. Your only option is to send it via regular or "snail" mail. Unfortunately, enemy spies at the post office have been opening and reading letters. How can you safely send your message? You can hide it under the envelope's stamp.

HERE'S WHAT YOU'LL NEED:

1) 1 pencil
2) 1 envelope
3) 1 roll of clear tape
4) 1 self-adhesive postage stamp still attached to its backing. (A "self-adhesive" stamp is like a sticker. It doesn't need licking or moistening.)

HERE'S HOW TO DO IT:

Don't peel the stamp away from its backing yet.

Place the stamp in the upper right-hand corner of the envelope and trace its outline with the pencil. Remove the stamp and write your message inside the box.

THIS IS
A SECRET
MESSAGE

Cut a clear piece of tape big enough to cover your message but small enough to stay inside of the box. Stick it over the message. Erase the outlines of the box.

Peel the stamp away from its backing and place it over the message. (The tape will act as a shield, allowing you to remove the stamp later without ripping the paper.) To read your message, all your fellow agent has to do is peel away the stamp.

TIP: You can also use this trick with normal stickers. If you need to get a message to a friend or fellow agent, you could hide words or letters under a series of stickers on a piece of paper. Just make sure that you put clear tape over each message so that the sticker won't rip the paper when it's peeled off.

11. MAKING MINIATURE MESSAGES

A microdot is a microscopic message hidden on a disc no bigger than the period at the end of this sentence. While you won't have access to a microdot-making machine, you can still practice the art of making miniature messages.

HERE'S WHAT YOU'LL NEED:

1) 1 sheet of plain paper
2) 1 computer with a word processing program like Microsoft Word
3) 1 clear marble, magnifying glass, or cell phone with a camera app
4) Scissors

HERE'S HOW TO DO IT:

Using your computer, type the message you want to send on a blank page. I'm going to use the following as my example:

Meet me in the park at 7 pm

Notice how the words automatically appeared in a size that was easy to read. Now, highlight the message and reduce its size. This is what it would look like if I reduced it to a font size of 5.

Meet me in the park at 7pm

This is a perfect size for miniature messages. It's almost two small for the naked eye to see, but a good enough size for a low-tech magnifying device to enlarge.

Print out your message onto a piece of paper. Use a magnifying glass, clear marble, or camera app on a cell phone to see which one magnifies the message best. Tell your fellow spy which one to use.

Once you've made your message, the final step is to deliver it. You could hide it under a sticker or postage stamp. Or, you could conceal it inside a fortune cookie.

Fortune cookies make excellent delivery devices. Just cut your message out into a thin strip of paper (like a fortune) and slip it inside. Leave the cookie somewhere for your fellow agent to find. To release the message, all your friend has to do is bite into the cookie!

12. HIDING MESSAGES IN A SUDOKU GRID

Earlier, you learned how to use an empty crossword puzzle to hide top secret messages. Now you can do the same with a sudoku grid.

		3		6				
	3	6		1	2			
9			5	8	6		4	
	9	7		3				4
	8			5		2		
	1	2				8	6	
	5						9	
				7	3		5	
7	4							2

FUN FACT: Sudoku is a popular puzzle game that originated in Japan in the 1980s. The objective of sudoku is to fill the spaces of a grid with the numbers 1 through 9, using each number only once in each row or column.

HERE'S WHAT YOU'LL NEED:

1) 1 unused sudoku puzzle grid
2) 1 pencil, pen, or marker
3) 1 piece of paper

HERE'S HOW TO DO IT:

Since sudoku is a game using numbers, you'll need to come up with a series of numbers that represent the letters of your message.

First, draw a railroad track with twenty-seven columns. Make sure that the first column is wider than the others. Draw a box around the track so that it resembles a chart.

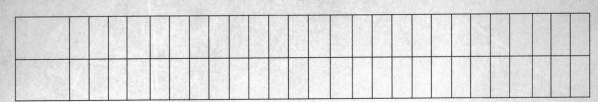

Next, write the word "Letter" in the upper left-hand box, followed by the letters of the normal alphabet ("A" to "Z"). Then, write the word "Number" in the first column of the second row, followed by the numbers 1 through 26.

Your chart should look like this:

Letter	A	B	C	D	E	F	G	H	I	J	K	L	M	N	O	P	Q	R	S	T	U	V	W	X	Y	Z
Number	1	2	3	4	5	6	7	8	9	10	11	12	13	14	15	16	17	18	19	20	21	22	23	24	25	26

Say you wanted to send the following message:

BE CAREFUL

First, find the letter "B" and the number underneath. It's 2. Write it down. Next, find the letter "E" and its number. It's 5. Write that number down too. Do this for the remaining letters in the message. Eventually, you'll get:

2, 5, 3, 1, 18, 5, 6, 21, 12

That's the number sequence for BE CAREFUL. Now fill in your sudoku grid.

Start with the upper left-hand square and write the numbers in from left to right. Repeat the sequence over and over again until all of the squares are taken. Skip the spaces that the puzzle maker has already filled in.

This is what your puzzle grid should look like:

2	5	3	**3**	1	18	**6**	5	6
21	**3**	**6**	12	**1**	**2**	2	5	3
9	1	18	**5**	**8**	**6**	**5**	**4**	6
21	**9**	**7**	12	**3**	2	5	3	**4**
1	**8**	**18**	**5**	**5**	**6**	**2**	21	12
2	**1**	**2**	**5**	**3**	**1**	**8**	**6**	18
5	**5**	**6**	21	12	2	**5**	**9**	3
1	**18**	**5**	**6**	**7**	**3**	21	**5**	12
7	**4**	2	**5**	**3**	**1**	18	5	**2**

To solve, all your fellow agent has to do is write down the letter that corresponds to each number from left to right. Eventually, he or she would get:

BECAREFULBECAREFULBECAREFULBECAREFULBECAREFULBECARE

Even though the letters run together and the last word is cut-off, the message is clear. You are telling someone to BE CAREFUL.

TIP: Make sure that your fellow agent knows to use only the handwritten numbers. If he or she uses the puzzle maker's numbers too, then the message won't make sense.

CIPHERS

Now that you've mastered steganography, aka the art of hiding top secret messages in or on things, it's time to apply your secret agent mind to ciphers.

A cipher is a cryptic message that uses other letters, numbers, or symbols for the letters of the original message. Writing ciphers might seem tricky at first, but they're actually easy once you get the hang of it. There are many different types of ciphers covered in this section. But you don't have to stick to these. You and your friends can have fun making up your own.

FUN FACT: A "cryptanalyst" is someone who deciphers or "cracks" ciphers or coded messages. Historical figures like Queen Elizabeth I of England, King Philip II of Spain, and Pope Clement VII were all known to have used cryptanalysts.

1. USING ANAGRAMS TO HIDE YOUR MESSAGES

Although not technically ciphers, anagrams are included in this section because they involve changing the order of the letters in a secret message in order to hide it.

While you may not have heard the word "anagram" before, you've probably solved one. Have you ever been to a restaurant and received a kids' activity sheet where you're asked to unscramble letters like the following?

KLMI

KLMI is the anagram. MILK is the answer.

Solving one-word anagrams is easy, but deciphering longer ones can be hard. That's why we can use them to conceal top secret messages.

HERE'S WHAT YOU'LL NEED:

1) 1 pen, pencil, or marker
2) Plain paper

HERE'S HOW TO DO IT:

Think of the message that you want to write. Scribble it on your sheet of paper. I'm going to send the following as my example:

BEWARE OF THE MAN WITH THE BLACK HAT

The next step is to scramble the letters of each word. Although there is no right answer to how you should jumble the letters, this is how I have chosen to do it.

RAWBEE FO EHT ANM TIHW ETH KALCB TAH

Anyone looking at that message would find it pretty tricky to solve.

But because it's not impossible to decipher, you might want to add an extra level of security. You could delete the spaces in between words.

RAWBEEFOEHTANMTIHWETHKALCBTAH

Now THAT'S a complicated-looking anagram!!

The only way to solve it would be to know:

1) That it's an anagram

2) How many letters are in each word of the message

To tell your friend or fellow agent that it's an anagram, you could let them know ahead of time, or include the letter "A" (for anagram) somewhere on the note.

You could include a number code on the piece of paper. Each number could stand for the number of letters in each word.

For example, the number code for BEWARE OF THE MAN WITH THE BLACK HAT would be: 62334353. There are 6 letters in the first word, 2 in the second, 3 in the third, and so on. You could write that code in the upper right-hand corner of the note.

To solve this type of anagram, all you'd have to do is separate the letters according to the number.

RAWBEE/FO/EHT/ANM/TIHW/ETH/KALCB/TAH

And then put them back in the correct order.

BEWARE/OF/THE/MAN/WITH/THE/BLACK/HAT

CRACK THE CODE!

Now that you understand how anagrams work, see if you can figure out what these anagrams are saying. Some of them are trickier than others because the spaces between the words are missing. For these, I have included a special code. Good luck!

SGRAAANM ERA UFN = _____

_____

TEA RUOY GTBLEVEASE = _____

_____

OD UYO VAEH A OGD? = _____

_____

THAWSIUROYVFAROETIRLOCO? (42485) = _____

_____

YMAVORFEITSIDER (2823) = _____

_____

2. CREATING AND DECIPHERING A ZIGZAG CIPHER

A zigzag cipher is a type of cipher created by writing the letters of your message on different lines and in alternating spaces. Some people call the zigzag cipher a "rail fence" cipher because the letters go up and down like the peaks of a white picket fence.

HERE'S WHAT YOU'LL NEED:

1) 1 pencil, pen, or collection of colored markers
2) Plain paper

HERE'S HOW TO DO IT:

Draw a line from left to right on your sheet of paper. Then add a bunch of vertical lines, leaving enough space in between them to fit a letter. It should look like a railroad track.

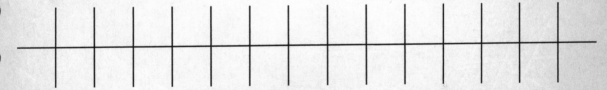

Next, decide what your message will be. As an example, I'm going to send this message to a fellow agent.

WAIT FOR MY SIGNAL

Write your "W" in the upper left-hand corner, and then fill in the rest of the letters, so that they zigzag up and down, up and down.

W		I		F		R		Y		I		N		L
	A		T		O		M		S		G		A	

To create the first half of your cipher, simply write down the letters from the top row.

WIFRYINL

Then add the letters from the bottom row IN A DIFFERENT COLOR.

WIFRYINLATOMSGA

The reason that I have used a different color for the second half is so that my cipher will be easier to decode.

To decipher the message, just reverse the process.

Draw another railroad track, filling in the letters from the first half of the cipher in the top row. Make sure to skip spaces in between.

W		I		F		R		Y		I		N		L

Then, add the letters from the second half of the cipher in the empty spaces on the TOP ROW ONLY.

W	A	I	T	F	O	R	M	Y	S	I	G	N	A	L

Voilà! You have deciphered your first zigzag cipher.

CRACK THE CODE!

See if you can crack the following zigzag ciphers. You will want to create a railroad track on a separate sheet of paper, so that you can easily solve them.

RGRHT**OETA** = _____

_____

WAAECA**ERRDOT** = _____

_____

MEANO**ETTON** = _____

_____

SCEAET**ERTGN** = _____

_____

CVRATO**OETCIN** = _____

_____

3. CREATING AND DECIPHERING A CAESAR CIPHER

Julius Caesar was famous for many things, including the development of his "Caesar cipher." As previously mentioned, the emperor replaced the letters of the alphabet with ones that were three places to the right. Even though Caesar lived a long time ago, we can still use his methods to disguise our messages.

Julius Caesar
(100–44 B.C.)

HERE'S WHAT YOU'LL NEED:

1) 1 pen, pencil, or marker
2) Plain paper

HERE'S HOW TO DO IT:

Draw a railroad track with twenty-seven columns. Make sure that the first column is wider than the others. Draw a box around the track so that it resembles a chart.

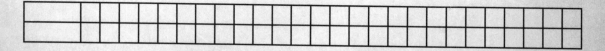

Next, write the word "Normal" in the upper left row, followed by the letters of the normal alphabet (from "A" to "Z"). Write the word "Caesar" in the first column of the second row, followed by the letters of the Caesar cipher alphabet. Remember, Caesar's alphabet started with a "D," three letters to the right of the "A."

Once you're done filling in your letters, it should look like this.

Normal	A	B	C	D	E	F	G	H	I	J	K	L	M	N	O	P	Q	R	S	T	U	V	W	X	Y	Z
Caesar	D	E	F	G	H	I	J	K	L	M	N	O	P	Q	R	S	T	U	V	W	X	Y	Z	A	B	C

Now you have the key for writing and solving any Caesar cipher.

Let's use the chart to write a Caesar cipher for:

ENEMY APPROACHING

First find the "E" in the "Normal" row, and look underneath it for its corresponding Caesar cipher letter, which is "H." Write that down. Next, look underneath the "Normal" letter "N." Its cipher letter is "Q." Write that down too. Eventually, we'd come up with the following:

HQHPB DSSURDFKLQJ

That's the Caesar cipher for ENEMY APPROACHING!

To decode a Caesar cipher, all you have to do is the reverse. Say you received the following message:

GRQW VDB DQBWKLQJ

Find the letter "G" in the "Caesar" row and look above it for the normal letter. It's "D." Write that down. Find the letter "R" in the "Caesar" row and look for the normal letter above it. The answer is "O." Eventually, you'll come up with:

DONT SAY ANYTHING

Even without the apostrophe between "N" and "T," you can understand the message. Decoding Caesar cipher messages is easy, if you have the secret chart.

CRACK THE CODE!

Now that you know how to write and crack Caesar ciphers, see if you can decode the following:

ORRN IRU WKH VHFUHW PHVVDJH = _____

_____

PB JDGJHW LV EURNHQ = _____

_____

VKH LV D VSB = _____

_____

FDQ BRX GHFLSKHU WKLV = _____

_____

GLVJXLVH BRXUVHOI= _____

_____

TIP: You don't have to stick to Caesar's idea of replacing letters with ones that are three places to the right. You could create a cipher alphabet using letters that are ten places to the right, or even five places to the left. Whichever way you decide, make sure that you create a new chart based on it and keep it handy.

4. CREATING AND DECIPHERING AN ATBASH CIPHER

An Atbash cipher is like a Caesar cipher in that it substitutes one letter for another. But with an Atbash cipher, the first letter of the alphabet ("A") is replaced with the last letter of the alphabet ("Z"). The second letter of the alphabet ("B") is replaced by the second to last letter ("Y"), and so on. Basically, it reverses the order of the English alphabet.

On the surface, Atbash ciphers seem like they'd be easy. After all, it's just the alphabet in reverse, right? But Atbash ciphers are REALLY tricky. Unless you know the key, they're almost impossible to figure out.

Take a look at this example.

> HSLFG RU BLF MVVW SVOK

Any idea what it says? Probably not. The only way to solve it is to learn the secret.

HERE'S WHAT YOU'LL NEED:

1) 1 pen, pencil, or marker
2) Plain paper

HERE'S HOW TO DO IT:

Draw a railroad track with twenty-seven columns, the first column wider than the others. Draw lines around the track so that it looks like a chart.

Second, write the word "Normal" in the upper left row, then the letters of the normal alphabet ("A" to "Z"). Next, write the word "Atbash" in the first column of the second row, followed by the Atbash cipher alphabet. Remember, the Atbash alphabet starts with "Z" and goes backward to "A."

Your chart should look like this.

Normal	A	B	C	D	E	F	G	H	I	J	K	L	M	N	O	P	Q	R	S	T	U	V	W	X	Y	Z
Atbash	Z	Y	X	W	V	U	T	S	R	Q	P	O	N	M	L	K	J	I	H	G	F	E	D	C	B	A

Now you're ready to write an Atbash cipher. Say for example, you wanted to send the following message.

THE CODE IS CORRECT

First, you'd find the letter "T" in the "Normal" row, and look underneath for the Atbash cipher letter. The answer is "G." Write it down. Next, find the "Normal" letter "H" and the Atbash letter underneath. The Atbash cipher letter is "S." Write it down too. If you continued writing the Atbash letters, you'd come up with:

GSV XLWV RH XLIIVXG

And that's the Atbash cipher!

To decode an Atbash cipher, just reverse the process. Say you received the following message:

HSLFG RU BLF MVVW SVOK

First, find the Atbash letter "H" and look above it for the "Normal" letter. It's "S." Next, find the Atbash letter "S" and look above it for the "Normal" letter. It's "H." Eventually, you'd come up with:

SHOUT IF YOU NEED HELP

And that's the decoded message!

CRACK THE CODE!

Now that you know how to write and crack Atbash ciphers, see if you can decode these secret messages using the chart on the previous page.

GSV VMVNB RH MVZI = _____

_____

NVVG BLF ZG GSV OFMXS GZYOV = _____

_____

YV XZIVUFO = _____

_____

SRWV GSV NVHHZTV RM BLFI SZG = _____

_____

R OLHG NB WVXLWVI YIZXVOVG = _____

_____

TIP: Once you feel ready, you can start using Atbash ciphers with friends and fellow agents. But make sure they have a copy of the chart too, or else they will find it too difficult to solve.

5. CREATING AND DECIPHERING A NUMBER CIPHER

With the zigzag, Caesar and Atbash ciphers, we learned how to replace the letters of our original message with new letters from a cipher alphabet. Now, we're going to learn how to replace letters with numbers to create a number cipher.

HERE'S WHAT YOU'LL NEED:

1) 1 pen, pencil, or marker
2) Plain paper

HERE'S HOW TO DO IT:

Draw a railroad track with twenty-seven columns. Remember to keep the first column wider than the others. Draw lines around the track so that it looks like a chart.

Second, write the word "Normal" in the upper left spot, followed by the letters of the alphabet ("A" to "Z"). Write the word "Number" in the first column of the second row, followed by the numbers 1 to 26.

Your chart should look like this.

Normal	A	B	C	D	E	F	G	H	I	J	K	L	M	N	O	P	Q	R	S	T	U	V	W	X	Y	Z
Number	1	2	3	4	5	6	7	8	9	10	11	12	13	14	15	16	17	18	19	20	21	22	23	24	25	26

Say I wanted to send the following message using a number cipher:

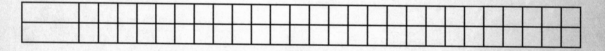

YOUR SECRET IS SAFE WITH ME

All I have to do is write the numbers that correspond to the letters in my message followed by a "."

First, find the letter Y in the "Normal" row, and look underneath it for its "Number." The number is 25. Write it down. Next, find the "Normal" letter "O" and its number underneath. It's 15. Write it down. Note that I have added a "." between each number. Eventually, you'd get:

25.15.21.18.19.5.3.18.5.20.9.19.19.1.6.5.23.9.20.8.13.5

The deciphered message would become:

YOURSECRETISSAFEWITHME

Even without spaces, you can tell what the message says.

CRACK THE CODE!

Now that you know how number ciphers work, see if you can decode the following number ciphers using the chart above. To make things easier, I have used a "/" to separate the words in each cipher:

25.15.21/1.18.5/2.5.9.14.7/23.1.20.3.8.5.4 = _____

8.5/9.19/1.14/5.14.5.13.25/1.7.5.14.20 = _____

20.8.9.19/9.19/20.8.5/4.18.15.16 = _____

9.20/9.19/4.5.3.12.1.19.19.9.6.9.5.4 = _____

13.25/7.1.4.7.5.20/9.19/19.1.6.5 = _____

Writing and cracking number ciphers is a lot of fun. But some people already know which letters correspond with which numbers. For example, most people know that A = 1, B = 2 and Z = 26. So they could quickly solve your number cipher.

To make things more difficult, you could add by 2's to change the numbers. Like this:

Normal	A	B	C	D	E	F	G	H	I	J	K	L	M	N	O	P	Q	R	S	T	U	V	W	X	Y	Z
Number	2	4	6	8	10	12	14	16	18	20	22	24	26	28	30	32	34	36	38	40	42	44	46	48	50	52

Or, you could start with a big number and subtract by 5s. Here's an example:

Normal	A	B	C	D	E	F	G	H	I	J	K	L	M	N	O	P	Q	R	S	T	U	V	W	X	Y	Z
Number	129	124	119	114	109	104	99	94	89	84	79	74	69	64	59	54	49	44	39	34	29	24	19	14	9	4

Ultimately, it's up to you. In fact, you could use a totally random collection of numbers! Either way, make sure to keep your chart handy so that your cipher will be easy to solve.

6. CREATING AND DECIPHERING A SYMBOL CIPHER

So far, we've learned how to substitute letters and numbers for the normal alphabet. Now, we're going to take a look at using symbols.

HERE'S WHAT YOU'LL NEED:

1) 1 pen, pencil, or marker
2) Plain paper

HERE'S HOW TO DO IT:

Just like we did with the previous ciphers, make a railroad track with twenty-seven columns and two rows.

Fill in the word "Normal" in the upper left column of the first row, then write the letters of the normal alphabet from "A" to "Z." Next, write the word "Symbol" in the second row on the left, and create twenty-six different symbols to represent the letters of the cipher alphabet. You can draw funny swirls as symbols or use symbols from a computer keyboard. I have used a combination of symbols and numbers from a keyboard in my example.

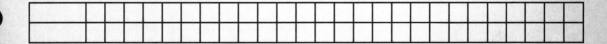

Normal	A	B	C	D	E	F	G	H	I	J	K	L	M	N	O	P	Q	R	S	T	U	V	W	X	Y	Z
Symbol	!	3	?	:	*	>	)	;	@	(	2	=	$	4	#	7	,	1	&	9	^	%	5	+	/	6

Say, I wanted to send the following message to my friend:

I AM HUNGRY

All I have to do is find the "Symbol" letter that is underneath my "Normal" letter and write it down. For example, the "Symbol" for the "Normal" letter "I" is @. The symbol for the "Normal" letter "A" is !.

If I were to write each symbol down, the cipher would become:

@ ! $; ^4) 1/

To decode a symbol cipher, all I have to do is reverse the process. If I was given:

>@*=: !)*49

I would write the "Normal" letter that matches each symbol one at a time. The resulting message would become:

FIELD AGENT

Couldn't be easier!

CRACK THE CODE!

Now that you know how to work with symbol ciphers, see if you can decipher the following symbol ciphers using my chart on p. 49:

$@?1#:#9& ! 1* 9@4/ = _____

&#$*#4* @& 5! 9? ; @4) = _____

?1/79#)1!7;/ @& >^4 = _____

5*!1 ! 5@) = _____

:# 4#9 &!/ ! 5#1: = _____

7. MAKING YOUR OWN DECODER BRACELET!

Now that you know how ciphers work, you can easily create a decoder bracelet for writing and deciphering them. That way, you don't have to lug this book around every time you want to send a message!

HERE'S WHAT YOU'LL NEED:

1) 1 piece colored paper card *

2) 1 ruler

3) 1 pencil

4) 1 hole puncher

5) 1 sheet of paper

6) 1 piece of string or ribbon

7) Scissors

* The card needs to be thin enough to bend around your wrist, but thick enough so that it won't easily tear. You could try regular paper, but it might rip.

A decoder bracelet

HERE'S HOW TO DO IT:

Cut a strip of card at least 1 inch (or 2.5 cm) thick and 6 inches (or 15.25 cm) long. Wrap the strip around your wrist to test the fit. Trim any excess paper off the ends.

Next, decide which substitution cipher you want to use. Leave a bit of space at the top and bottom of the paper, and draw a vertical line down the middle. Add twenty-five horizontal lines across the center line. (This is a vertical version of the railroad track we used in earlier sections.)

Write the "normal" alphabet in the left-hand column and your cipher alphabet in the right. I'm going to use a Caesar cipher that starts five places to the right, so my cipher alphabet will start with an "F." Here's what my decoder bracelet would look like:

Use your hole puncher to punch a hole at the top and bottom of your strip. (Make sure that you don't accidentally punch a hole through any of your letters!)

To finish off your bracelet, thread a piece of string or ribbon through the holes and tie it around your wrist. Now you have a decoder bracelet that you can take with you everywhere you go.

ALTERNATE PROJECT:

You could use these same instructions to make a decoder ring! All you have to do is use a smaller, thinner strip of card and write your letters really small. To fasten it, just wrap a piece of clear tape around your "ring." This will keep the paper together and protect your letters from rubbing off at the same time.

A	F
B	G
C	H
D	I
E	J
F	K
G	L
H	M
I	N
J	O
K	P
L	Q
M	R
N	S
O	T
P	U
Q	V
R	W
S	X
T	Y
U	Z
V	A
W	B
X	C
Y	D
Z	E

Wear them anywhere!

TIP: To quickly and easily share messages with your friend or fellow agent, you should create a pair of matching decoder bracelets or rings!

8. MAKING YOUR OWN ALBERTI CIPHER WHEEL

In 1466, a man named Leon Battista Alberti developed a device that could more easily make (and break) substitution ciphers. It was called the Alberti cipher wheel.

The Alberti cipher wheel contained two discs, one inside the other. The inside disc contained the cipher alphabet, while the outer disc had the normal alphabet. The inner and outer discs were like the top and bottom rows of our railroad tracks. But with the Alberti cipher wheel you could actually MOVE the discs, changing the cipher alphabet whenever you wanted. That meant the person developing the ciphers could stay one step ahead of the enemy.

You can use the principles of Alberti's device to create your own cipher wheel.

Leon Battista Alberti
(1404–1472 A.D.)

HERE'S WHAT YOU'LL NEED:

1) 2 circles (1 small and 1 large). You can either trace the ones on the next page, or make a photocopy of them.
2) 1 pen or marker
3) 2 pastel colored pencils or crayons
4) 1 paper fastener, sometimes called a "brad"
5) 1 paper clip
6) Scissors

Alberti's
cipher wheel

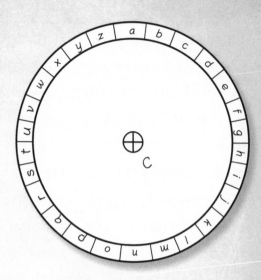

HERE'S HOW TO DO IT:

Once you've copied them, cut out both circles. The bigger wheel represents your "normal" alphabet. The smaller wheel is the "cipher" alphabet. So that you can remember which is which, you might want to color them different colors. Or, you could put a "C" in the middle of the smaller wheel for "cipher."

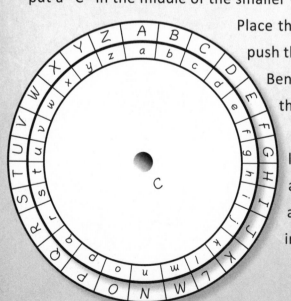

Place the smaller disc on top of the bigger one, and push the paper fastener through the center of both. Bend the prongs at the back of the larger disc so that the two circles are not fastened.

This is what your cipher wheel should look like. The two discs should be able to move around freely. If not, spin the paper fastener around a bit, so that it makes more of a hole in the center of the paper.

To write a cipher using your wheel, all you have to do is:

1) Set the wheel according to your key
2) Decide what your message will be
3) Write down the "cipher" letters that are underneath your "normal" letters

To set your wheel, turn the inside disc until you reach your key. By "key," I mean the rule for creating and solving your cipher.

I'm going to use a key of "six places to the right of the normal alphabet" as my example. So, I have to turn the inside disc six places TO THE LEFT until the cipher "G" is under the normal "A."

If my key was "three places to the left," then I would turn the inner wheel three spaces TO THE RIGHT, so that the "X" was under the "A."

After aligning the letters, fasten the discs together with a paper clip.

Now that my wheel is set, it's time to come up with my cipher. I want to send the following:

IT IS RAINING OUTSIDE

With the cipher wheel, it's easy. All I have to do is find each letter from the original message on the outside wheel and write down the cipher letters that appear underneath.

In my example, the "O" is underneath the letter "I." The "Z" is under the letter "T." The "O" is under the letter "I." And so on. So, my cipher is:

OZ OY XGOTOTM UAZYOJK

Notice how I have kept the spaces in between. This is so that it will be easier to solve later on. But if I wanted to make it trickier, I could delete the spaces and then write a number code (like we did in the "Anagram" section) on the note that would tell my friend or fellow agent how many letters were in each word. The number code for my example would be 2277.

2277

OZOYXGOTOTMUAZYOJK

Then, all they would have to do is separate out the cipher accordingly.

OZ/OY/XGOTOTM/UAZYOJK

After writing out the normal letters, eventually you'd come up with:

IT IS RAINING OUTSIDE

And that's the message!

TIP: You'll want to make sure that your friend or fellow agent has an identical cipher wheel, so that you can make and decipher each other's message more easily.

CRACK THE CODE!

See if you can use my key above (six places to the right) to decipher the following wheel ciphers:

HK IGXKLAR = _____

_____

JU TUZ ZXAYZ NOS = _____

_____

HOTGXE IUJK = _____

_____

QKKV UAZ = _____

_____

CNGZ OY ZNK VGYYCUXJ = _____

_____

9. CREATING AND DECIPHERING A GRID CIPHER

So far, we have been creating ciphers by putting the letters of the normal and cipher alphabets into a chart or by organizing them onto a wheel. Another way to create a cipher is to arrange the letters of the alphabet into a square grid with six rows and six columns. This kind of cipher is called a "grid cipher" or a "Greek square."

HERE'S WHAT YOU'LL NEED:

1) 1 pen, pencil, or marker
2) Plain paper

HERE'S HOW TO DO IT:

Draw a grid with six rows and six columns. Leave the top left space empty, and write numbers 1 through 5 across the top row and down the first column.

The headings of your grid should look like this.

	1	2	3	4	5
1					
2					
3					
4					
5					

Next, fill in the letters of the normal alphabet from top to bottom, starting with column 1. Since there are twenty-six letters of the alphabet and only twenty-five spaces, Y and Z will share the last space. Here's what your grid should look like.

	1	2	3	4	5
1	A	B	C	D	E
2	F	G	H	I	J
3	K	L	M	N	O
4	P	Q	R	S	T
5	U	V	W	X	Y/Z

To write a cipher using this grid, all you need to do is write the row number followed by the column number for each letter. Make sure that the row number comes first. Here's an example.

Say I wanted to write the following phrase:

MISSION COMPLETE

"M" is located in the box where row 3 and column 3 meet. So, its number is 33. "I" is located at the intersection of row 4 and column 2. So, its number is 42. "S" is in row 4 and column 4. So its number is 44.

The grid cipher for MISSION COMPLETE would be:

33, 42, 44, 44, 42, 53, 43/ 31, 53, 33, 14, 23, 51, 54, 51

Notice that I have used a "," to separate the letters and a "/" to separate the words.

To solve for it, all I have to do is to find the letter in the row and column hinted at by each "number." The number 33 tells me that I need to look in row 3, column 3. The letter there is an "M." Row 4, column 2 tells me the second letter is an "I." And so on. Eventually, I'd get:

MISSION COMPLETE

Writing grid ciphers is easy, huh?

CRACK THE CODE!

Now that you know how to use the grid, see if you can solve the following ciphers.

31, 42, 14, 32, 51, 34 = _____

44, 14, 55/ 22, 23, 11, 44, 44, 51, 44 = _____

22, 11, 41, 22, 51, 54 = _____

51, 43, 51, 33, 55 = _____

21, 53, 53, 21, 55, 54, 34, 11, 14 = _____

10. MAKING AND BREAKING A TIC-TAC-TOE CIPHER

The tic-tac-toe cipher, also known as a "pigpen" cipher, is a substitution cipher that replaces letters with symbols. The symbols, however, don't come from a computer keyboard like with the symbol cipher in this manual. They're created by placing the twenty-six letters of the alphabet into four grids, and putting dots next to thirteen of the letters. Two of the grids look like Xs; while the other two look like tic-tac-toe boards. Thus, the name.

HERE'S WHAT YOU'LL NEED:

1) 1 pen, pencil, or marker
2) Plain paper

HERE'S HOW TO DO IT:

On your first sheet of paper, draw two empty tic-tac-toe grids and two cross grids. This is what your grids should look like.

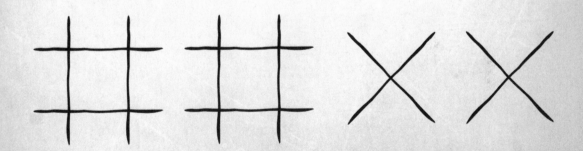

Now, fill in the letters of the alphabet starting with "A" in the upper left space of the first tic-tac-toe grid. Carry on writing your letters from left to right in each grid

71

until all of the spaces are filled.

Put a dot next to the letters in the 2nd and 4th grids. You can put your dots anywhere you like, but they're best next to the letter, a line or where two lines meet.

Take a look at my example.

See how I've placed my dots near intersecting lines and only on two grids? Make sure that you do that too.

Now that your grids are filled out, it's time to make your key. Use a second sheet of paper to write the alphabet vertically, i.e. from top to bottom. Put an equal sign next to each letter like this.

A =
B =
C =

And so on.

Next, draw the symbols associated with each letter. The symbols are the lines and dots next to each letter. Sometimes, it's only lines. Sometimes, it's a combination of dots and lines. None of the symbols include the letter itself.

For example, surrounding the letter "A" are two lines that meet at a right angle.

So, that is the symbol for "A."

Surrounding "N" is a box of lines with a dot underneath the letter. This is the symbol for "N."

N = ⊡

If I were to fill in the symbols for the rest of the letters based on my examples above, my tic-tac-toe cipher alphabet would look like the chart on the right.

Of course you might want to put your letters and dots in totally different places, and that's OK. The most important thing is that each letter be given its own unique symbol.

Now that you've developed your key, you can start writing (and solving) tic-tac-toe ciphers.

Let's practice by writing the phrase TIC TAC TOE. All you have to do is write the symbols for each letter, leaving a space in between. This is how TIC TAC TOE would look as a cipher:

If you wanted to make it trickier for someone to solve, you could leave out the spaces. Or, put nulls in between.

To decipher a tic-tac-toe cipher, all you have to do is reverse the process. Look up the symbols, and write the letters that correspond to them.

What do you think this cipher says?

>E⅂ V▢L⌐▢>

It says:

TOP SECRET

CRACK THE CODE!

Use the key on the previous page to solve these tic-tac-toe ciphers.

⅃⌐⅂ <E< ⌐⌐▢⅃ >∩▢ L⅃<▢?

<V▢ >∩▢ VL<>⅃⌐▢

>∩▢ ▢<⅃⅃ ⌐V ⅃

LE<▢> >E >▢▢

>∩▢ V▢U ⅃L⅃▢VV LE⅃▢
⌐V V<⅂▢⌐ V⅂<

FUN FACT: Tic-tac-toe ciphers were used by secret societies of men in England about 500 years ago and during the American Civil War 150 years ago.

TIP: If you give someone a tic-tac-toe cipher, make sure they have a copy of your alphabet or else they won't be able to solve it.

11. USING A VIGENÈRE TABLE TO CREATE A CIPHER

In 1586, a man named Blaise de Vigenère developed a system for creating an unbreakable cipher. His key was to use a secret keyword in combination with a table of 676 letters. This table showed the alphabet written 26 times, each time starting with a different letter. Vigenère's table was used for many centuries.

Without knowing the keyword AND the message, Vigenère ciphers are pretty impossible to solve. In fact, it's the most secure (and complicated) method for writing ciphers in this book. No one will be able to crack it!

Blaise de Vigenère
(1523–1596 A.D.)

HERE'S WHAT YOU'LL NEED:

1) Copy of Vigenère's table (next page)
2) 1 pen, pencil, or maker
3) Plain paper

HERE'S HOW TO DO IT:

First, take a look at Vigenère's table (on the next page). Notice how there are two headings, one on each side of the table. One says "message" the other says "KEYWORD." You will learn how to use these headings later on.

Now, take a look at the capital letters INSIDE the table. Look at them from left to right. Notice how with each row, the alphabet starts with a different letter. The first row starts with an "A" and ends with a "Z." The second starts with a "B" and ends with an "A." The third starts with a "C" and ends with a "B," and so on. Each row is like a new Caesar cipher. But instead of moving the alphabet over three places, Vigenère moved it over by one space per row.

message

	a	b	c	d	e	f	g	h	i	j	k	l	m	n	o	p	q	r	s	t	u	v	w	x	y	z
A	A	B	C	D	E	F	G	H	I	J	K	L	M	N	O	P	Q	R	S	T	U	V	W	X	Y	Z
B	B	C	D	E	F	G	H	I	J	K	L	M	N	O	P	Q	R	S	T	U	V	W	X	Y	Z	A
C	C	D	E	F	G	H	I	J	K	L	M	N	O	P	Q	R	S	T	U	V	W	X	Y	Z	A	B
D	D	E	F	G	H	I	J	K	L	M	N	O	P	Q	R	S	T	U	V	W	X	Y	Z	A	B	C
E	E	F	G	H	I	J	K	L	M	N	O	P	Q	R	S	T	U	V	W	X	Y	Z	A	B	C	D
F	F	G	H	I	J	K	L	M	N	O	P	Q	R	S	T	U	V	W	X	Y	Z	A	B	C	D	E
G	G	H	I	J	K	L	M	N	O	P	Q	R	S	T	U	V	W	X	Y	Z	A	B	C	D	E	F
H	H	I	J	K	L	M	N	O	P	Q	R	S	T	U	V	W	X	Y	Z	A	B	C	D	E	F	G
I	I	J	K	L	M	N	O	P	Q	R	S	T	U	V	W	X	Y	Z	A	B	C	D	E	F	G	H
J	J	K	L	M	N	O	P	Q	R	S	T	U	V	W	X	Y	Z	A	B	C	D	E	F	G	H	I
K	K	L	M	N	O	P	Q	R	S	T	U	V	W	X	Y	Z	A	B	C	D	E	F	G	H	I	J
L	L	M	N	O	P	Q	R	S	T	U	V	W	X	Y	Z	A	B	C	D	E	F	G	H	I	J	K
M	M	N	O	P	Q	R	S	T	U	V	W	X	Y	Z	A	B	C	D	E	F	G	H	I	J	K	L
N	N	O	P	Q	R	S	T	U	V	W	X	Y	Z	A	B	C	D	E	F	G	H	I	J	K	L	M
O	O	P	Q	R	S	T	U	V	W	X	Y	Z	A	B	C	D	E	F	G	H	I	J	K	L	M	N
P	P	Q	R	S	T	U	V	W	X	Y	Z	A	B	C	D	E	F	G	H	I	J	K	L	M	N	O
Q	Q	R	S	T	U	V	W	X	Y	Z	A	B	C	D	E	F	G	H	I	J	K	L	M	N	O	P
R	R	S	T	U	V	W	X	Y	Z	A	B	C	D	E	F	G	H	I	J	K	L	M	N	O	P	Q
S	S	T	U	V	W	X	Y	Z	A	B	C	D	E	F	G	H	I	J	K	L	M	N	O	P	Q	R
T	T	U	V	W	X	Y	Z	A	B	C	D	E	F	G	H	I	J	K	L	M	N	O	P	Q	R	S
U	U	V	W	X	Y	Z	A	B	C	D	E	F	G	H	I	J	K	L	M	N	O	P	Q	R	S	T
V	V	W	X	Y	Z	A	B	C	D	E	F	G	H	I	J	K	L	M	N	O	P	Q	R	S	T	U
W	W	X	Y	Z	A	B	C	D	E	F	G	H	I	J	K	L	M	N	O	P	Q	R	S	T	U	V
X	X	Y	Z	A	B	C	D	E	F	G	H	I	J	K	L	M	N	O	P	Q	R	S	T	U	V	W
Y	Y	Z	A	B	C	D	E	F	G	H	I	J	K	L	M	N	O	P	Q	R	S	T	U	V	W	X
Z	Z	A	B	C	D	E	F	G	H	I	J	K	L	M	N	O	P	Q	R	S	T	U	V	W	X	Y

KEYWORD

Once you understand how the table is set up, you can move to the next step which is picking a keyword.

Your keyword could be anything. It could be a color (like "blue" or "magenta"), a silly word (like "achoo" or "yikes"), or something to do with your message (like "mission").

Third, you need to decide what your message will be. It can be anything, but the shorter the better.

Now that you have both your keyword and message, you'll need to write them down. BUT they need to be written down in a particular way.

Draw a railroad track with two rows and a number of columns. Make sure that you have enough columns to fit your message. If, for example, your message contains twenty letters, you'll need to make sure that you have twenty columns.

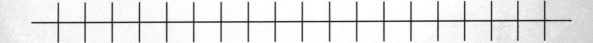

Next, write your message (without spaces in between the words) in lowercase letters on the bottom row. I'm going to use "BEWARE OF THE MAN IN RED" as an example. Don't forget to write your letters in lowercase. This is a really important step.

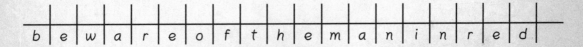

| b | e | w | a | r | e | o | f | t | h | e | m | a | n | i | n | r | e | d |

After writing your message, it's time to write the keyword. Write your keyword in capital letters on the top line over and over again until you run out of space. My keyword is going to be "SPY." Remember to use capital letters only for the keyword.

| S | P | Y | S | P | Y | S | P | Y | S | P | Y | S | P | Y | S | P | Y | S |
| b | e | w | a | r | e | o | f | t | h | e | m | a | n | i | n | r | e | d |

With this railroad track, you have the "key" for writing a Vigenère cipher.

Remember how there were two headings on the table on page 66. One said "KEY-WORD" in CAPS on the left, and the other said "message" at the top in lowercase letters.

Find the capital "S" on the KEYWORD side and run your finger across the "S"-row until you're in the "b"-column. (Remember, the "S" was in the top row of your railroad track and the "b" was at the bottom.) The point at which the "S"-row and the "b"-column meet is the letter "T." So, that's the first letter of your cipher.

Now, do the same for "P." The point at which the "P"-row and "e"-column meet is at the letter "T" too. So that's the second letter of your cipher.

Next, find the intersection point for the letter "Y"-row and the "w"-column. It's at the letter "U."

So far, the cipher is "TTU."

If you were to finish writing it out, the cipher for "BEWARE OF THE MAN IN RED" would be:

TTUSGCGURZTKSCGFGCV

Unless someone had a copy of your keyword and the table, there is almost no way that they could solve this cipher! (By the way, it doesn't matter that your cipher doesn't contain spaces. In fact, it makes it harder to solve.)

To solve a Vigenère cipher, all you have to do is the reverse.

Draw a railroad track, and put your keyword at the top again. But this time, instead of writing the message at the bottom in lowercase letters, write your cipher in capital letters.

S	P	Y	S	P	Y	S	P	Y	S	P	Y	S	P	Y	S	P	Y	S
T	T	U	S	G	C	G	U	R	Z	T	K	S	C	G	F	G	C	V

Now, go back to the "S"-row in the KEYWORD section. Starting at the "S," run your finger across that row until you hit the capital letter "T" inside the table. Then, look at which letter is at the top of that column. In this case, it's the letter "b." That's the first letter of your message.

Run your finger from the letter "P" to find the second letter "T" from your cipher. It's in the "e"-column.

Doing the same thing from the letter "Y," you'll find the letter "U" in the "w"-column. That's the third letter.

So far, you have:

> bew

If you were to keep writing the letters down, you'd come up with:

> bewareofthemaninred

And that's the message!

CRACK THE CODE!

Now that you know how to work with Vigenère ciphers, see if you can decode these messages. I have put the keyword in parentheses. For example, (SPY). Remember to draw your railroad track and put your keyword across the top row in capital letters and either your message (in lowercase to create a cipher) or a cipher (in capital letters to solve a cipher) in the bottom row.

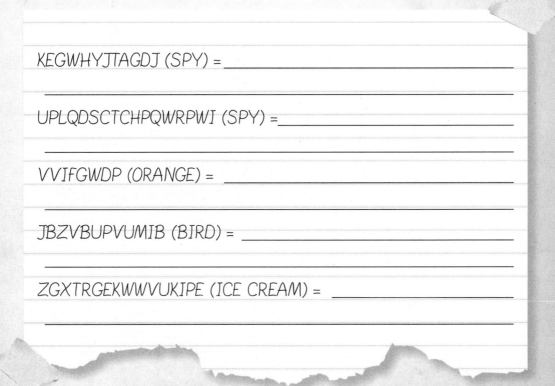

KEGWHYJTAGDJ (SPY) = _____

_____

UPLQDSCTCHPQWRPWI (SPY) = _____

_____

VVIFGWDP (ORANGE) = _____

_____

JBZVBUPVUMIB (BIRD) = _____

_____

ZGXTRGEKWWVUKIPE (ICE CREAM) = _____

_____

Now see if you can create Vigenère ciphers using these messages and keywords:

Don't tell anyone (STAR)

Your secret is safe (RED)

Hide this message (AGENT)

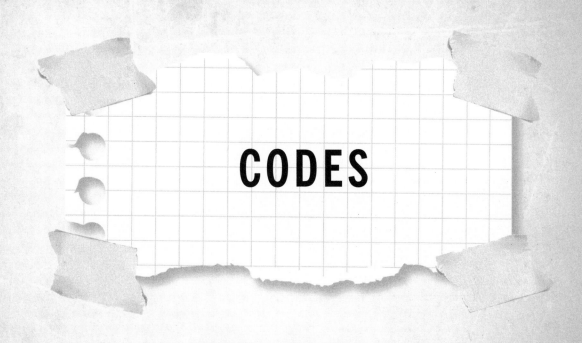

CODES

A code is a symbol, action, word, or phrase that stands for something else. For example, the US Secret Service uses the code name "Air Force One" to refer to the president of the United States' airplane. They called President Obama "Renegade" and Queen Elizabeth II "Kitty Hawk." But it's not just secret service agents and spies that use codes. Believe it or not, you and I use codes on a daily basis.

Have you ever sent a text to someone using the letters "LOL"? That's code for "laugh out loud." What about an emoticon? Sending a smiley face to tell someone you're happy is another way of sending a coded message.

If you become a spy or secret agent when you're older, you'll probably be asked to memorize lots of codes and code names. But for now, you can use some already existing codes to send your top secret messages. Keep reading to find out how . . .

1. KNOCKING OUT A SECRET MESSAGE

Pretend that you and a fellow agent have been captured by the enemy. You're being held in separate rooms with a wall in between you. You need to tell her something, but there's a guard sleeping outside your door. How can you talk to her without speaking? You could knock out a message on the wall using the "tap code."

HERE'S WHAT YOU'LL NEED:

1)   1 copy of a Greek square (see below)

HERE'S HOW TO DO IT:

Take a look at the following chart. The letters of the alphabet are arranged in a grid with five rows and five columns. This is the same "grid cipher" or "Greek square" used in the cipher section, except that in this method, the "C" and the "K" share a square (instead of the "Y" and "Z").

	1	2	3	4	5
1	A	B	C/K	D	E
2	F	G	H	I	J
3	L	M	N	O	P
4	Q	R	S	T	U
5	V	E	X	Y	Z

To send a message using this Greek square, all you have to do is "tap" or "knock out" the row number of the letter, followed by its column number.

For example, say you wanted to send the message "HELP."

The letter "H" is in row 2, column 3. So, all you have to do is knock two times, briefly pause and then knock three more times. For "E," knock once, pause, and then knock five more times. And so on.

If your fellow agent has a copy of the chart (or has memorized it) he or she will be able to quickly pick up on the message. Make sure to pause longer between letters than you do between row and column numbers. That way your fellow agent knows when a new letter starts.

Since the tap code is specific to the English language, it's an excellent way to communicate in enemy territory where English isn't the primary language.

FUN FACT: The tap code was used among prisoners of war during the Vietnam War and World War II as a way to communicate and keep up morale.

2. USING BRAILLE TO DISGUISE MESSAGES

Braille is a coded system of raised dots specially designed for blind people so that they can read and write using their fingertips. It was named after its creator, a French man named Louis Braille. Braille was born with sight but he had an accident when he was three years old and lost his ability to see. Louis came up with the idea of using raised dots to represent letters when he was a teenager. Raised dots meant that instead of reading each letter, blind people could *feel* them. In 1837, Braille's work was published and the Braille system was made available to the world.

Louis Braille
(1809–1852 A.D.)

Today, Braille is used on everything from pedestrian crosswalk buttons to elevators to toilet signs to railroad signs and even to wedding rings. But because most of the world is unaware of how to read Braille, you can use it as a way to send messages. Obviously, your dots won't be raised but the arrangement of dots is what you can use.

HERE'S WHAT YOU'LL NEED:

1) 1 pen, pencil, or marker
2) Plain paper

HERE'S HOW TO DO IT:

This is the Braille alphabet.

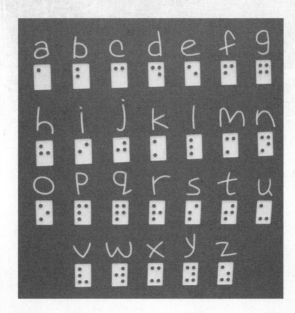

See how each letter has its own unique arrangement of dots? To send a coded message using Braille, all you have to do is copy the dot combinations for each letter of your message.

For example, the word "AGENT" would be written like this:

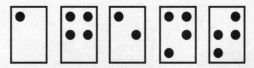

To decipher a Braille message, all you have to do is look at your chart and write down the letters that match the symbols.

Take a look at this coded message.

If you look up each symbol and write down its corresponding letter, you come up with the message "ENIGMA."

Pretty easy, huh?

CRACK THE CODE!

See if you can decode these coded messages written in Braille.

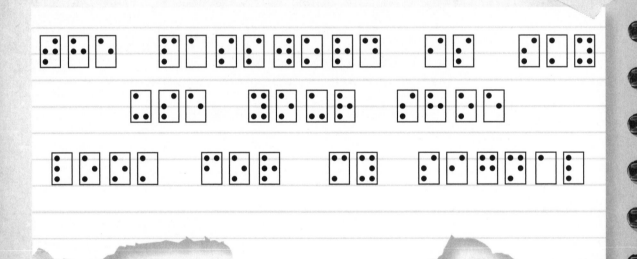

3. USING MORSE CODE TO CONCEAL MESSAGES

In the "History of Cryptography" section, we learned about an American inventor named Samuel Morse. In 1832, Morse came up with the idea of a single-wire electric telegraph that could send messages around the world using sounds to stand for letters. This coded alphabet became known as Morse code

Although Morse code isn't a secret, many people still don't know how to use it. That means you can rely on it to send your top secret messages. You can use Morse code to write messages, flash them with a flashlight, tap them onto a wall, or spell them out by blinking your eyes.

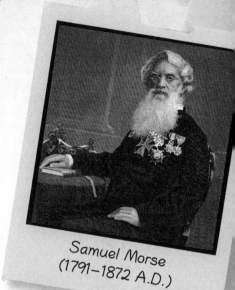

Samuel Morse
(1791–1872 A.D.)

HERE'S WHAT YOU'LL NEED:

1) 1 pen, pencil, or marker

2) Plain paper

3) Optional: flashlight or walkie-talkie

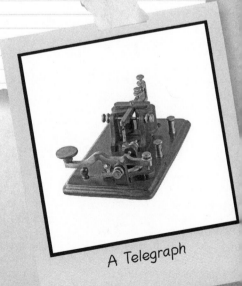

A Telegraph

HERE'S HOW TO DO IT:

This is Morse code.

See how there is a unique series of dots, dashes, or combination of the two for each letter? To write it, all you have to do is copy the dot and dash combinations for each letter in your message.

Say, I wanted to write the word "Help." To write the "H," I just copy down the four dots for "H." It would look like this:

A	• —		U	• • —
B	— • • •		V	• • • —
C	— • — •		W	• — —
D	— • •		X	— • • —
E	•		Y	— • — —
F	• • — •		Z	— — • •
G	— — •			
H	• • • •			
I	• •			
J	• — — —			
K	— • —		1	• — — — —
L	• — • •		2	• • — — —
M	— —		3	• • • — —
N	— •		4	• • • • —
O	— — —		5	• • • • •
P	• — — •		6	— • • • •
Q	— — • —		7	— — • • •
R	• — •		8	— — — • •
S	• • •		9	— — — — •
T	—		0	— — — — —

• • • •

To add the "E," I would add another dot. Since I don't want to confuse the four dots of "H" with the one dot of "E," I should add a "/" between the letters. Like this:

• • • •/ •/

If I were to keep going, the word "Help" would be coded as:

• • • •/ •/ • — • •/ • — — •

If you wanted to write a message with more than one word, you could insert a "//" between the words. Here's what "Check for fingerprints" would look like:

—•—•/ • • • •/ •/—•—•/—•—// • •—•/————/ •—•// • •
—•/• •/—•/——•/ •/ •—•/ •——•/ •—•/ • •/—•/—/ • • •

The only drawback to using Morse code is that writing it takes up a lot of space.

You could also send a message using a flashlight. Say I wanted to send the message "Hi." Written out, the message would look like this:

• • • •/ • •

Since "Hi" is a combination of four short dots fol-lowed by another two short dots, you could flick a flash-light on and off four quick times, then pause for a second or so (to show that it's the start of a new letter), then flick it on and off two more quick times.

Walkie-talkies (even toy ones) emit a beeping sound when you push the talk button. You could use this to your advantage and send a message using Morse code.

For "Hi," just push the button down four quick times, pause for a second or so, then push the button again for another two.

Finally, you can tell someone "Hi" using your eyes. Just close them four fairly quick times, followed by a brief pause, and then close them another two.

Using Morse code is fun and easy!

CRACK THE CODE!

Decode the following Morse code messages:

—•—• / ——— / —•—• / —•—• / • / —•—• / —• // — / • • • • / • // —•

• / ——— / — / • • • = _____

_____

• • / —• // • • • • // —— / • • / —• / • • — / — / • / • • • = _____

_____

TIP: You might want to go slowly if you're using flashlights, walkie-talkies or your eyes to send a Morse code message. Sometimes it takes time and practice for other people to understand it.

CERTIFICATE OF
ACHIEVEMENT

Awarded to

_____

for completing

BASIC CODE-BREAKING TRAINING

This ____ day of ____ in the year ____

CRYPTOGRAPHIC CHALLENGE

CONGRATULATIONS!

You've reached the end of the book and are ready to test your newfound skills with the Cryptographic Challenge! This master quiz puts together many of the techniques that you learned into a series of coded messages. Solve them all to reveal an important message about becoming a secret agent.

To help, there's a hint before each code telling you what kind of technique was used. For example, the first coded message was created using the "Bump and Shift" method. If you need help solving it (or any of the messages), all you have to do is refer to that section of the book.

Good luck!

Elizabeth Singer Hunt

CRYPTOGRAPHIC CHALLENGE

(Bump and Shift)

    T OBECOM E ASECRE TAGEN TYO UMUS TD O WEL LI NSCHOO L

(Anagram: 10, 8, 4, 3, 3, 3, 3, 4, 2, 4, 6, 3, 5, 4, 11, 10, 3, 7, 9)

    ETVRGOMNENCGEASINEKIELHETACIDAN6IMKIELOTRHEILEPOPEH

    WODUTSYATMHERGNGEIENINYGHECTONOLNADGINFEORSGELNAGUA

(Atbash cipher)

    DSROV HLNV ZTVMGH YVXLNV HKRVH LGSVIH DLIP RM LUURXVH

(Caesar cipher: Three spaces to right of normal alphabet)

    EHLQJ DEOH WR ZRUN LQ WHDPV DQG NHHS VHFUHWV DUH

    LPSRUWDQW VNLOOV WR KDYH

(Backward spelling)

    STNEGA DEEN OT EB YLLACISYHP TIF DNA OT EB ELBA OT KLAT OT SREHTO

(Zigzag cipher)

    MNAETAELOXETDORVLHWRDAYGNSRASEPCETTAETEOL

(Anagram: 5, 1, 6, 5, 2, 4, 4, 3, 2, 3, 4, 2, 3, 3, 9)

    GEBNIACTREESNGATESIRAHDKORWTBUTIACNOLASEBNUFNDAWDRAEIGNR

(Vigenère: Keyword SPY)

    QDSOXJDBYCTLWLDJXCFSQOWGDTFWANACELDIWTNQDSJRMMCRJNQSUC

GLOSSARY

Anagram A word or phrase whose letters are jumbled.

Cipher A type of message that substitutes new letters, numbers, or symbols for the letters of an original message.

Code A type of message that uses signals, words, or phrases to stand for something else.

Cryptanalyst Someone who tries to decode or break a secret message.

Cryptography The art of writing and breaking secret messages. The word comes from the Greek words *kryptos* meaning "secret" or "hidden" and *graphein* meaning "to write."

Encryption The process by which messages are concealed.

Secret Agent A person employed by a government or agency that is tasked with, among other things, gathering confidential intelligence information.

Spy A person who gathers confidential information about another person or organization without permission. A spy may or may not be employed by a government or agency.

Steganography The art of concealing messages in or on something else. The word comes from the Greek words *steganos* meaning "covered" and *graphein* meaning "to write."

ANSWER KEY

BACKWARD SPELLING: page 18

OD UOY EVAH RUOY YPS SESSALG = DO YOU HAVE YOUR SPY GLASSES

EKAM ERUS OT RAEW PUEKAM = MAKE SURE TO WEAR MAKEUP

TAHW EMIT LLIW EHT EGAKCAP EVIRRA = WHAT TIME WILL THE PACKAGE ARRIVE

TI SI NEDDIH EDISNI EHT NEP = IT IS HIDDEN INSIDE THE PEN

ESU ELBISIVNI KNI = USE INVISIBLE INK

BUMP AND SHIFT: page 27

TH EP APER SAR EI NTH EBRIEFCAS E = THE PAPERS ARE IN THE BRIEFCASE

H EI S ARUSSIA NSP Y = HE IS A RUSSIAN SPY

8SH 8EWIL 8LMEE 8TYO 8UI 8NTH 8EPAR 8K = SHE WILL MEET YOU IN THE PARK

2TH 2EPLAN 2EWIL 2LLAN 2DA 2T7 = THE PLANE WILL LAND AT 7

2TRAININ 2GSTART 2SA 2T1 21 = TRAINING STARTS AT 11

ANAGRAMS: page 46

SGRAAANM ERA UFN = ANAGRAMS ARE FUN

TEA RUOY GTBLEVEASE = EAT YOUR VEGETABLES

OD UYO VAEH A OGD? = DO YOU HAVE A DOG?

THAWSIUROYVFAROETIRLOCO? (42485) = WHAT IS YOUR FAVORITE COLOR?

YMAVORFEITSIDER (2823) = MY FAVORITE IS RED

SYMBOL CIPHERS: page 60

$@?1#:#9& ! 1* 9@4/ = MICRODOTS ARE TINY

&#$*#4* @& 5!9?;@4) = SOMEONE IS WATCHING

?1/79#)1!7;/ @& >^4 = CRYPTOGRAPHY IS FUN

5*!1 ! 5@) = WEAR A WIG

:# 4#9 &!/ ! 5#1: = DO NOT SAY A WORD

ALBERTI WHEEL CIPHER: page 67

HK IGXKLAR = BE CAREFUL

JU TUZ ZXAYZ NOS = DO NOT TRUST HIM

HOTGXE IUJK = BINARY CODE

QKKV UAZ = KEEP OUT

CNGZ OY ZNK VGYYCUXJ = WHAT IS THE PASSWORD

GRID CIPHERS: page 70

31, 42, 14, 32, 51, 34 = CIPHER

44, 14, 55/ 22, 23, 11, 44, 44, 51, 44 = SPY GLASSES

22, 11, 41, 22, 51, 54 = GADGET

51, 43, 51, 33, 55 = ENEMY

21, 53, 53, 21, 55, 54, 34, 11, 14 = BOOBYTRAP

TIC-TAC-TOE CIPHERS: page 74

ꓩᒋꓶ ᐊᴇᐸ ᒥꕔꓕꓩ ＞ꓵꓳ ꒒ꖬᐸꓳ? = DID YOU FIND THE CLUE?

ᐸᴠꓳ ＞ꓵꓳ ᴠꓶᐸ＞ꓩꓶꓶꓳ = USE THE SCYTALE

＞ꓵꓳ ꓳᐸꓶꓶ ꓛᴠ ꓕ = THE NULL IS A

101

LE<Ɋ> >E >ɊɊ = COUNT TO TEN

>ɊɊ VɊU JLLɊVV LEJɊ
ΓV VㄑꓞɊΓ Vꓞㄑ = THE WEB ACCESS CODE IS SUPER SPY

VIGENÈRE CIPHERS: page 80

KEGWHYJTAGDJ (SPY) = Spies are cool

UPLQDSCTCHPQWRPWI (SPY) = Can you keep a secret

VVIFGWDP (ORANGE) = He is a spy

JBZVBUPVUMIB (BIRD) = It is a mystery

ZGXTRGEKWWVUKIPE (ICE CREAM) = Retrace your steps

Don't tell anyone (STAR) = VHNKLXLCSGYFFX

Your secret is safe (RED) = PSXIWHTVHKMVJEIV

Hide this message (AGENT) = HOHRMHOWZXSYETX

BRAILLE: page 88

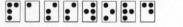

= THE PASSWORD IS SKY

= USE YOUR SHOE

= LOOK FOR MY SIGNAL

MORSE CODE: page 92

—•—•/———/—•/—•/ •/—•—•/—//—/• • • •/ •//—• •/———/—/ • • •

= CONNECT THE DOTS

• •/—•// • • • •/ •//——/ • •/—•/ • •—/—/ •/ • • • •

= IN 5 MINUTES

To become a secret agent you must do well in school

Government agencies like the CIA and MI6 like to hire people who study math engineering technology and foreign languages

While some agents become spies others work in offices

Being able to work in teams and keep secrets are important skills to have

Agents need to be physically fit and to be able to talk to others

Many agents are also expected to travel the world

Being a secret agent is hard work but it can also be fun and rewarding

You will make new friends while helping to keep your country safe